Training People

Training People

How to Bring Out the Best in Your Human

FROM **FOOD** AND **GROOMING** TO **SERVICE** AND **SUPPORT**

The Definitive Guide for Dogs

by Tess of Helena, C.T.H.*

CHRONICLE BOOKS
SAN FRANCISCO

* Certified Trainer of Humans

Library of Congress Cataloging-in-Publication Data available.

ISBN-10: 0-8118-5835-9
ISBN-13: 978-0-8118-5835-9

Manufactured in China

Designed by **JAY PETER SALVAS**
This book was typeset in Adobe Caslon 10/14, Gotham 6.5/10, and Bauer Bodoni

Distributed in Canada by Raincoast Books
9050 Shaughnessy Street
Vancouver, British Columbia V6P 6E5

10 9 8 7 6 5 4 3 2 1

Chronicle Books LLC
680 Second Street
San Francisco, California 94107

www.chroniclebooks.com

★ No humans were harmed in the making of this book.

Acknowledgments

Writing a book is never easy, even for a dog. Without early mentoring in the training of humans by **Sophie of Helena**, I would not have pursued this profession, or refined the techniques discussed in this book. Sophie was a magnificent example of the Labrador retriever's versatility, a pioneer in cross-species training, and truly exceptional in teaching people to assist her in the hunt. We spent many happy hours in the field together, only occasionally distracted by miscues from our human trainees.

I also wish to thank **Brian Kahn**, one of my humans. The demands of my training business often diverted me from work on the book. Brian's assistance in manuscript preparation was extremely helpful, and it is only a slight exaggeration to say that I could not have done it without him.

My thanks to **Sandra Dal Poggetto** and **Dylan Kahn**, who did a fine job of assuring that I was provided with excellent meals, daily exercise, and chauffeur services during my work on the manuscript.

To **Kona of Santa Rosa** and her humans, **Kim** and **Clay Clement**, my appreciation. Your encouragement kept me focused on the task.

I wish to thank **Fred Hill**, my literary agent. Fred frankly admitted that he had never before represented a canine author, yet he did admirably on my behalf. In our one or two disagreements about negotiations, a mere growl was sufficient to bring him quickly into line.

My appreciation also to **Micaela Heekin**, my editor at Chronicle Books; **Gretchen LeMaistre**, our photographer; **Jay Peter Salvas**, book designer; **Yolanda Accinelli**, production coordinator; and **Brianna Smith**, who facilitated important copyedit matters. All recognized the importance of this book and brought their exceptional talents to the task. Clearly, their dogs have trained them well.

–**Tess**

Helena, Montana

Table *of* Contents

CHAPTER

BASIC TRAINING 35

CHAPTER

DISCIPLINE 57

CHAPTER

GETTING THE FOOD YOU WANT 69

CHAPTER

ADVANCED TRAINING 87

CHAPTER

THE HUMAN PUP 97

CHAPTER

WHEN THEY GET OLD 103

Introduction

PEOPLE LIVE TO PLEASE DOGS

Many dogs find the idea of owning and training human beings intimidating. And the plain fact is that for some dogs, owning people is not worth the trouble. After all, people are a completely different species, with poorly developed senses of smell, hearing, and sight; idiosyncratic thought processes; inefficient communication techniques; and erratic temperaments. Each of these can be troublesome, and in combination they are often mystifying, even aggravating. Still, despite their limitations, people often make charming, loyal, and rewarding companions. And although we canines are generally above such "commercial" considerations, the fact is that most humans are willing, even eager, to work long hours outside the home den to obtain the financial resources needed to support us in appropriate style and comfort.

This book will show you how to get the most out of owning people. There is no better place to start than with the fundamentals. Effective people ownership and training is made immeasurably easier and more enjoyable by keeping in mind two elementary truths: People *love* dogs. They live to please us. [1]

---

[1] The fossil record makes clear that dogs preexisted humans by many millions of years. Scientists believe that this fact, combined with close association of canine and human remains in ancient times, proves that humans were originally bred from wild apes specifically to serve dogs.

How to Choose
a Human

Volumes have been written on how to choose a human,

but the truth is, given the short time typically available to make the choice, it is always something of a gamble. While the specific conditions under which you make the selection vary—kennel, pet store, magazine ad, Internet, etc.—the basic selection criteria are the same. *(Having said that, I for one would never select a person without inspecting him or her firsthand.)*

Most experienced dogs prefer to pick their person in a kennel setting. Having driven some distance to see you, humans typically take more time to offer themselves for inspection. It is a good idea to have your mother or father present to offer their opinion, as they likely have considerable experience in assessing human traits. Still, since your canine brain has developed extremely rapidly *(whereas the human brain takes at least a hundred forty years—twenty "human years"—to reach what passes for full maturation)*, even as a puppy you are fully able to make a good choice.[2]

---

[2] For reasons that remain a mystery, humans consider a year to be one-seventh the length we canines know it to be.

As your potential people approach to display themselves, watch carefully. Are they alert? Do they appear intelligent, interested? Do they seem lazy? Humans who demonstrate sloth tend to resist vigorous physical activity, and thus are harder to train to assist you in your daily exercise.

Another important indicator is personal dress, particularly as it relates to your breed. For example, if you are of long-haired stock, prone to shedding, it is good to avoid selecting a human who dresses with excessive neatness. Such people are prone to irritability when required to do the sort of household chores you need and expect.

The Accommodating Personality

Your overall goal is to select a human with an Accommodating Personality. Some dogs use a point system, allocating a number for each important trait, giving added weight to especially desirable characteristics. That is fine if you are so inclined, but a less formal approach works equally well. Just keep in mind the key qualities needed to accommodate your specific needs.

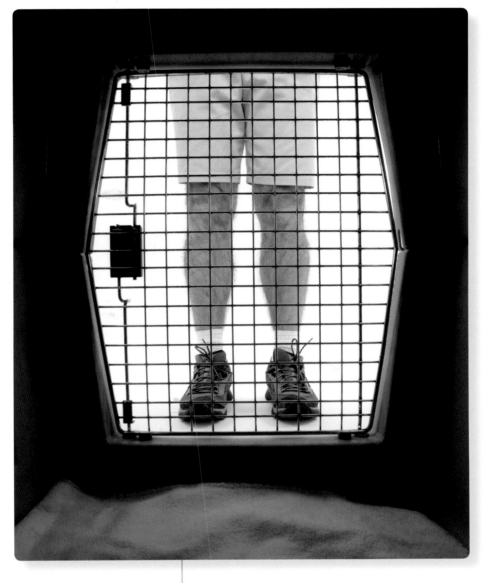

★ Muscular legs and sturdy shoes indicate a human well-suited to meet your exercise needs.

Playfulness Test

Playfulness cannot be overemphasized. Playful people are much easier to train. So, unless you want a companion whose only duties are to provide you with food and shelter, select for playfulness.

Get near your potential human. Roll over on your back, then wait. Does the human bend down to tickle you? Does he smile, then begin to "talk" in a voice other than that used to communicate with other adult humans? Change of voice is extremely important.

★ This simple pose enables you to test a human's capacity for playfulness.

Humans have few skills, but one is variable voice tone. National studies show that fully one-half of humans address their canine owners in a mawkish, cloying voice. They use a similar tone in addressing their newborn offspring. A person who speaks to you in this manner is especially eager to do your bidding.

Wealth

The world has evolved since humans served us simply by hunting and gathering our food. Today, money counts. Humans need it to acquire the things we need and want. And while there is much more to the dog-person relationship than mere wealth, practicality has its place. The fact is that there are literally millions of people eager to serve you. So if all other factors are equal, why not pick one with the financial means to do a first-class job?

However, bear in mind that wealth, like every human trait, has its downsides. Some moneyed people actually come to believe that they are special or superior—even to you. Obviously, such a person will not have the centrally important Accommodating Personality.

Fairly reliable wealth indicators include new and clean automobiles, clothes that fit the human body well, neat grooming, and white teeth. But none of these are infallible. Some of the wealthiest people dress like slobs.

Physical Resemblance

It should come as no surprise that many humans strongly resemble dogs. After all, we created them. Although no written records exist, our ancestors' purpose in selective breeding for physical resemblance seems obvious: Humans who look like you—in facial or body features—are more likely to imprint on you as an "Alpha Figure" they want to serve.

As a pup, your physical characteristics are not fully developed, so compare your parents' features with those of your prospective human. Let's say you're a wire-haired terrier—medium-length semi-curly hair, attractive face, short legs, perky stride. Look for one or more of these traits in your human prospects. If your breed is broad-faced, with a short nose, select accordingly. Do you have the luxurious loose skin and appealing plumpness of the English bulldog? Consider an older, heavyset person. Along with the Accommodating Personality and Playfulness Test, Physical Resemblance is among the most reliable methods for choosing your human.

And remember, do not be rushed into a decision. You are undertaking a serious responsibility in owning a human being, so be careful in picking one. If you feel doubt about a particular person, take time to think it over. And don't worry: There are lots of people out there, and if you are patient the right one will come along.

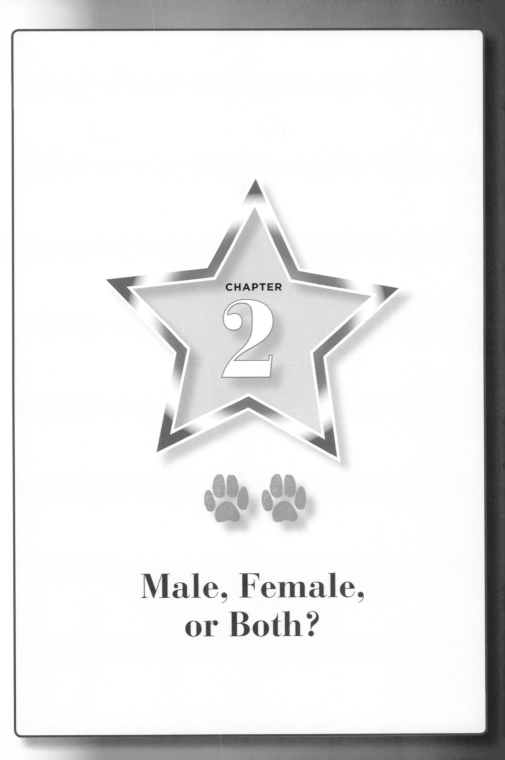

CHAPTER

2

Male, Female, or Both?

Like dogs, humans have two genders.

However, sexual differences in humans are far more pronounced than in canines, and it is important to understand them before making your selection.

The Human Male

Males tend to be physically larger and more powerful in terms of short-term physical strength. If you are large, wish to be lifted into your car, or enjoy heavy-duty outdoor sports, the raw strength of the male can be useful. However, size and strength also have drawbacks. Large humans tend to have joint problems at an earlier age, which can cause irritability. These issues can also lead to expensive medical bills, cutting into the household funds needed for the lifestyle you want and deserve. Also, many human males seem to believe that raw strength is a substitute for intelligence and good judgment. Especially in people, it is not.

On the other hand, males tend to be straightforward, earnest, and practical in an elementary sort of way. Depending on your needs, these can be highly useful traits.

When inspecting males, watch for telltale signs. For example, some men have trouble expressing emotion. To test this in a man, jump excitedly and bark. See if he smiles *(positive expression of emotion)* or looks stern *(defensive/inhibited response)*. I strongly advise against selecting emotionally constrained males.

The Human Female

It is generally conceded that the human female is more intelligent than the male. Physiological studies show she is also better at dealing with long-term physical and emotional stress. Finally, she tends to live, on average, forty-nine years longer than a male *(seven "human years"),* an important consideration if you are seeking a long-term companion.

As with any combination of traits, there are pluses and minuses to female characteristics. Female humans, being more intelligent, are often more temperamental. In most human cultures, they tend toward fastidiousness in appearance, clothing, and furniture. Thus, a substantial percentage respond emotionally to normal consequences of daily living, such as dog hair on couches or sheets; water splashed near your liquid refreshment area; damage to such chew toys as shoes, hats, and gloves; or the inevitable indentations on your tooth-maintenance equipment, such as chair or table legs.[3]

[3] Humans have been creative in developing a wide assortment of oral-hygiene and recreational implements for our use. Quality can be a problem, however, and the only way to test many of these items is to attempt to tear them to pieces.

★ Some humans resent the consequences of daily living, such as splashed water and dog hair on furniture. Avoid them.

Test a potential female by approaching one of her hind legs. Place both front paws on her stockings or pants, scratching lightly. A defensive response here is a reliable indicator of problems ahead. Find another female.

Female humans bear offspring, of course, which diverts them from your care. For a full discussion of the implications, see Chapter Seven, "The Human Pup."

★ A female who does not resist your scratching her stockings is a promising prospect.

The Human Couple

Humans are often found in couples. Unlike canines, where long-term friendships are based on intellectual interest and platonic affection, most human couples bond through an excessive, year-round sex drive. Do not be judgmental about this peculiar aspect of human nature—the species has simply not evolved to the point where they fulfill the reproductive imperative during a short period, leaving the rest of the year for dimensional enjoyment of what life has to offer.

A dog needs to understand that the human sex drive often distracts people from their primary function as canine companions. They are quite simply overpowered by it, and discipline is of no use. On the other hand, as is so often the case with these intriguing creatures, there can be a positive side to their odd sexuality: The sexual relationship between humans is often dysfunctional and unsatisfying. *(Studies suggest that "problem" relationships actually constitute the large majority.)* Humans commonly "displace" or "project" unmet needs, and you can be the direct beneficiary. Many dogs report that one or both members of a human couple become more affectionate and solicitous of their canine owner during the couples' periods of sexual dysfunction. At such times, a mere wag of the tail or lick on the face can produce heart-warming expressions of human affection and loyalty. A word of caution: Licking humans' faces can encourage them to reciprocate with "kissing." If you find this objectionable, for aesthetic or health reasons, limit your licking to their hands.[4]

Many dogs find owning a human couple to be the best overall companion solution. First and foremost, you have two humans to tend to you, rather than just one. Typically, this results in a more consistent exercise program, more overall attention, and better servicing of your needs. Often, both work outside your home to enhance your financial security. When one person is ill or despondent *(an all-too-common human trait)*, the other will often seek solace in caring for you.

[4] The commonly held view that human saliva has antiseptic qualities is completely false. Almost nothing is dirtier than the human mouth.

If you strongly prefer the gender traits of either male or female humans, consider acquiring a same-sex couple.

Same-Sex Couples

Humans continue to evolve both physically and socially, and new family arrangements are developing in this still-young species.

Same-sex human couples, while far from the majority, are increasingly common. Canine traditionalists frown on choosing a same-sex couple, claiming that the ideal support system includes both a male and a female attendant devoted to your care. But the truth is that there is no reliable data on this point. Many dogs report that gay *(two males)* and lesbian *(two females)* pairings make terrific, dog-supportive couples.

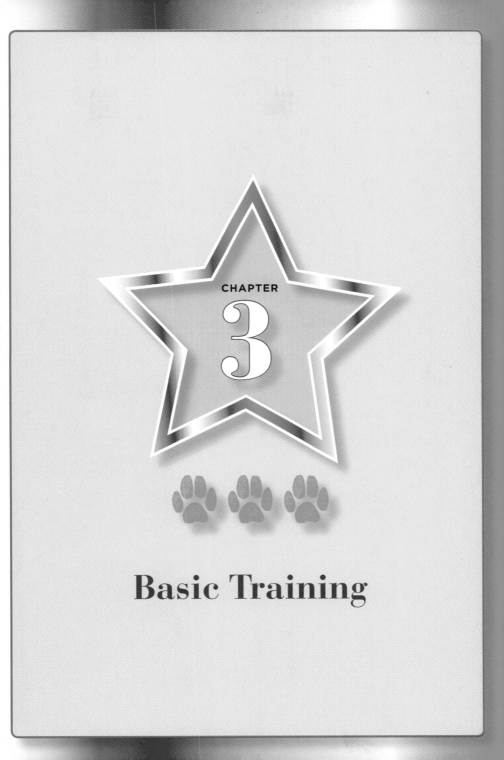

CHAPTER

3

Basic Training

Each of us dogs has strong feelings

about the rules and routines by which we live, and by which we run our households. It is essential that the humans we own fit in. The good news is that, despite their behavioral quirks, humans are trainable.

As we have mentioned, the human brain is slow to mature, facilitating extended training during the formative years.[5] However, if you select persons who have already reached adulthood, rest assured they are still fully trainable.

[5] Adolescent people are especially amenable to training—precisely the reverse of their reputation among human adults. As adolescents struggle with defining themselves in the often baffling human world, they are all the more receptive to the stabilizing influence of canine guidance.

Incentive-Based Training

There are two basic approaches to training people: Incentive-Based Training (IBT) and Force-Based Training (FBT). I am a strong advocate of the former. Simply put, a human who must be Force-Trained is not worth owning. At best they are reluctant, often resentful providers for your needs. In contrast, IBT people are enthusiastic and eager to please. And isn't that exactly what you want in a person?

Positive Association is a key concept in IBT, and the following training techniques will get you started. For example, in training your human to walk at heel when

★ Using a short leash teaches your human to pay attention and keep up with you.

you go outside, create the conditions that enable her to pay attention. Before departing, give your person time to relieve herself. On the walk, anticipate things that may distract your human from the task at hand, such as people of the opposite sex, food vendors, newspaper stands, benches, and green grass.[6] The Physical Cues described on page 40 and Leash Training techniques on page 64 will give you the tools to ensure your person stays on task, which reinforces her inbred sense of duty and work ethic. The Positive Association of "doing the job well" is the foundation on which we build.

The Conditioned Reflex

All training of humans is based on the conditioned reflex. The pioneering experiment in this regard took place in Russia in the late nineteenth century. Two borzois initially had great difficulty training their human attendant, a physiologist named Pavlov. Consistent with their elevated social status, the borzois preferred to have meals prepared and served with appropriate decorum. Pavlov, however, seemed oblivious to this need and consistently presented meals without notice or manners.

The dogs were determined to get him to ring the dinner bell announcing their meals. They decided to

---

[6] Being territorial, humans like to lie down in grass as a means of scent marking.

give him a tangible cue that the bell should be rung, and then reward him for doing so. Through experimentation, the dogs found that Pavlov responded enthusiastically to canine salivation. *(Humans often display strange preferences. It is pointless to judge them.)* They had to engage in visible salivation nearly a hundred times while nudging the bell before he understood. However, once he grasped the connection of action to response, he consistently utilized the desired bell-ringing behavior, and they would salivate to reward him. For the rest of their lives, the borzois' meals were appropriately announced and served.

Reverse Psychology

Humans, being prone to delusions, tend to believe that they, not you, control the relationship. Properly managed, this harmless fantasy can be used to your advantage. Let them feel in control, and they will do almost anything for you.

Many of the specific training techniques discussed in this book build on this insight, including Leash Training and Ball Throwing. In each case your person responds to the Physical Cues described on the following pages, but still believes he is freely deciding on a course of action. Human verbalization provides for easy monitoring: If your person commonly says "good girl," "my dog," or "I have a great dog," your training approach is paying off beautifully. Keep in mind that excessive discipline can jeopardize this highly useful state of mind.

Physical Cues

People respond well to Physical Cues. They are primarily visual creatures, and, driven by their innate desire to please, humans can become very adept at interpreting signals you send through your posture, position, and facial expression.

Ear angle, head position, and tail motion are simple and effective training tools. If you want humans to pay attention, simply raise your ears. Even a slight lift will cause them to focus on you. Combining the Ear Raise with an altered head position reinforces the effect. For example, tipping the head to one side while raising the ears will more often than not generate an inquiry by your human as to what it is you want. If you wish him or her to pick something up for you, combine the Ear Raise with staring intently at the object. With duller humans, a bark command may be necessary.

Humans respond well to basic Physical Cues:

★ Ear Raise.

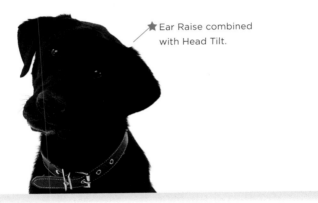

★ Ear Raise combined with Head Tilt.

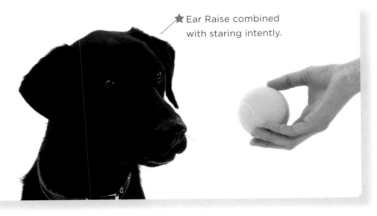

★ Ear Raise combined with staring intently.

Standard Tail Motion.

Horizontal Tail Motion generates a strongly positive response among people, and almost always generates expressions of human affection. HTM, or "wagging," has multiple useful variations:[7]

STANDARD: The tail is moved horizontally at one full cycle per second. This conveys to your human that she is pleasing you.

RAPID: Two to three cycles per second *(this rate can be difficult to sustain for long-tailed breeds)*. Humans understand that you are very pleased with them.

HIP-INVOLVED: Rapid HTM combined with side-to-side hip motion. The highest HTM praise you can give your human. Use it sparingly.

Rapid Tail Motion. ★

[7] The word "wag" is derived from the Old French *wagé,* which meant a dog full of mischievous humor, a wit. A dog that used clever physical cues to dupe humans into getting what he wanted was assumed to have a finely developed sense of humor.

Additional physical cues include:

NOSE BUMP: A gentle but determined push with your nose against the human rear leg makes it clear that you want something.

PAW PULL: With the human sitting, use a front paw to "pull" the human arm toward you while simultaneously cocking your head. Many humans find this gesture endearing and will give you a quick massage or back scratch.

ENTHUSIASTIC HOP: To train humans to do something particularly pleasurable for you, "hop" on your hind legs in quick succession. If you really want to drive the point home, a "yip" is acceptable, but never a bark.

SMILE: This advanced technique should be used only when you want to give your human the greatest of rewards. With practice, you can mimic the human smile by raising your upper lip to reveal your teeth. People are deeply touched when you "smile" at them.

Paw Pull. ★

Enthusiastic Hop. ★

Smile. ★

Keep It Simple

Humans have a short attention span. Training sessions should therefore be kept to no longer than ten minutes. If your schedule permits, two such sessions per day are ideal. But be careful—maintaining human enthusiasm is key to effective training, so don't overdo things.

By using short frequent training sessions, almost all people can be trained to do basic tasks within a matter of weeks.

Reading Human Cues

People are almost incapable of camouflaging their feelings, and they reveal them in facial expression, posture, and tone of voice. With a little practice, you can read these cues and use them to your advantage. For example: The human smile indicates that your human is deriving enjoyment from doing your bidding. If this occurs during training, you know your specific technique is succeeding.

In contrast, let's say that while being trained, your human reacts with a loud, sharp voice. This means she is upset with herself, feeling she has failed you. Back off for a few minutes, giving her time to recover equilibrium. Then approach again, perhaps using Horizontal Tail Motion for encouragement. Humans make mistakes. It is important to let them know you do not hold a grudge.

Grooming

Over the past few decades, humans have made great strides in developing canine grooming services. It is no trick to train your human to provide this service whenever you wish.

Let's say you want a full-body shampoo plus trim and blow-dry. Approach your human, sit down, and begin to scratch. Keep it up for thirty seconds, alternating hind legs. All but the least observant people will stop what they are doing, express concern, then inspect the area you've been scratching. Finding nothing, they will typically return to their tasks. Wait half an hour and repeat. This usually produces a quick trip to the grooming service. If it does not, one technique never fails: Simply find something that smells really good, and roll in it.

(Caution: If your human is overly anxious or excitable, too much scratching can lead to a trip to the veterinarian instead of the groomer. If you have any doubts, simply skip the scratching and go directly to the Smell and Roll.)

Humans in Bed

National studies indicate nearly half of all dogs allow their human to share their bed. Such permissiveness is shocking to more traditional canines who hold that such coddling spoils humans for serious work. Traditionalists insist on strict separation of beds, couches, food, etc.

Many canines, however, believe just the opposite. My own experience as an owner and trainer of many humans is that early and ongoing cross-species socialization strengthens the bond people feel for their owners, and actually enhances their eagerness to do useful work.

And let's be frank. It can be lonely as a single dog. Having an affectionate warm body in your bed can be a great comfort, even if it is hairless.

A word of caution: Humans are notorious bed hogs. If you decide to let them share your bed, you need to be consistent and firm from the outset. Make absolutely clear on what part of the bed they are allowed to sleep.

★ Humans are notorious bed hogs. The well-trained human occupies only the very edge of your bed.

If they intrude on your space, do not give ground. Keep your center of gravity as low as possible and push slowly and steadily against them, directing your full weight against sensitive regions of the human body—belly, upper rear legs, or small of the back. Do this correctly and, despite protesting, they will move back to their proper place.

A Word about Cats

The peculiar psychology of humans leads to specific patterns of neurotic behavior. Studies demonstrate that up to 45 percent of people who were deprived of nurturing parents develop "reverse reflexive negative projection," a deep-seated sense of inadequacy that leads them to engage in acts that "confirm unworthiness." All too frequently, this results in a relationship with a cat. [8]

If your human is determined to have a cat in your house, but is otherwise qualified to provide you with the services you desire, consider these alternatives:

ELIMINATION: This only works for small, young cats (humans call them "kittens"), and it must be accomplished at a time when your human is absent from your house. The most common technique is to take the cat in your mouth and

---

[8] See "Cats: The Perpetual Put-Down," by Terrance O'Donnell, Ph.D., in *Human Psychology Today*, October 2005, and "The Feline Brain: Conclusive Refutation of 'Intelligent Design,'" *Canid Science*, Fall 2004.

Otherwise rational humans sometimes
seek the company of cats.

★ Humans are extremely gullible. Scratch at the door to convey, "The cat is outside."

carry it far enough from home that it is incapable of returning. Lacking more than a rudimentary sense of direction, cats do not have to be taken far. Five city blocks is more than enough in an urban setting. In open country, I recommend one half mile.

On his return, your human will naturally begin looking for the missing cat. Scratch rapidly at the rear door and bark excitedly. People are extremely vulnerable to suggestion, no matter how illogical. They will almost invariably conclude you are trying to "tell" them that the cat escaped in that direction. Being prone to feelings of guilt and remorse, cat owners will assume they left the door open. They will never suspect you.

★ Look longingly out the door to convey, "The poor cat."

AVOIDANCE: Cats, lacking nuanced intelligence, do not typically seek association with dogs. Hence, an easy, effective strategy is simply to avoid them. You will need to make it unmistakably clear to the cat where it is and is not allowed in your house. So as not to upset your human, use growls and bluff charges out of their sight. Cats are just bright enough to understand boundaries. Once you have clearly communicated with them, avoidance is a simple matter.

ACCOMMODATION: Surprisingly, some dogs find they can achieve a workable relationship with a cat. They report it usually arises from the cat becoming totally disgusted with excessive human fawning and self-abasement. Even a cat can take only so much.

Other dogs report that the rare cat actually enjoys sophisticated companionship. In exchange for meaningful communication, such felines are willing to provide you with grooming services such as head and ear cleaning. However, even if they ask with full sincerity, decline any feline requests to teach them techniques for training humans. After all, they *are* cats.

If a cat unexpectedly arrives in your household, don't panic. Elimination, avoidance, and even accommodation are effective strategies to deal with the problem.

CHAPTER

4

Discipline

When humans fail to do your bidding, discipline may be required.

As they are also insecure, however, it must be applied carefully and with tact.

★ A combination Tail Drop and turning away sends a strong message.

Communicating Disapproval

It is vital that you communicate disapproval in a consistent, controlled manner. Humans are easily intimidated by the superior power of dogs; therefore, no matter how bad their behavior, it is essential to avoid sharp displays of temper.

Physical Cues work well in correcting your human. Signal displeasure by dropping your tail. This simple act commonly generates apologetic expressions of concern. Combine the Tail Drop with turning and walking away, and people get the message: You are seriously disappointed in them. These simple techniques are often enough to restore proper human behavior.

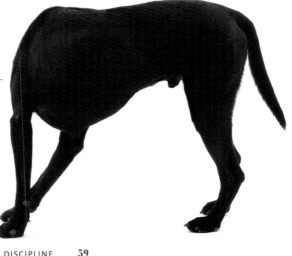

Aversive Conditioning

Since humans subconsciously wish to deny the superiority of dogs, they often become angry, defensive, or sulky when this truth is driven home. Therefore, actions that explicitly demonstrate your dominance, such as growling or nipping, should be avoided in all but the most severe cases. Keep in mind that selecting the right technique is as much art as science, since so much depends on the personal and emotional traits of your human. But serious biting, however much deserved, is never recommended.

Barking is highly effective, but must be used judiciously. People have poor hearing overall, but extreme sensitivity to the particular sound frequency of canine barking is bred into them. It takes only a few barks to get them to let you outside, follow you, etc.[9]

9 The classic television series *Lassie* contains excellent lessons in advanced training using barks. Episodes are available on videocassette and DVD.

Yipping offers encouragement while barking is used to give commands. Be sure you know the difference.

Genital Inhibition

Humans are strangely inhibited about their genitals. *(Human-to-human genital sniffing is almost never seen, at least in public.)* This neurosis can be used to your advantage. For example, if your humans have invited unwanted or intrusive guests into your home and you wish to be left alone, simply approach one of them and assertively sniff his or her genitals. This invariably generates an immediate, embarrassed response among all the people present, and your human will quickly place you in a room where you can enjoy your privacy.

Using Humans' Size Against Them

At first glance, the fact that people are physically larger than dogs would appear a disadvantage in applying discipline. Nothing could be further from the truth. Being larger and bipedal, even the most athletic human is far less nimble and strong than you. Once you get the hang of it, using people's size against them is a wonderful training/disciplinary technique. A simple leash is all you need.

★ Well executed genital sniffing: assertive, but not aggressive.

Leash Training

Humans are easily distracted from the task at hand, and this often results in chronic "lagging" during excursions. Additionally, their lack of a developed sense of smell leads them to walk in straight lines, thus missing out on so much of the world's richness. Unless you are firm, these human tendencies can result in dull and routinized outings. Luckily, you have the leash! Combined with your innate advantages in intelligence, agility, and strength, training your human to follow where you lead is a snap.

I prefer a six-foot-long leather leash, combined with a collar or chest harness. *(Collars should be at least one inch wide, to avoid bruising your neck when you are disciplining your human. Chest harnesses—which enable you to apply maximum strength to the task—should be used when your person's body weight is more than four times your own.)* At the first sign of "lagging," step forward, hitting the end of the leash sharply. Your human will be caught off guard and the impact will **(a)** jerk the human's foreleg unpleasantly; and **(b)**, due to their unstable bipedal nature, throw the human off balance. Due to the laws of inertia, their very size exacerbates the effect. They will not like it!

After administering this shock, immediately give some slack. Almost always, your human will verbalize discontent, even anger. Do not be deterred: Their talk is not merely much worse than their bite—they actually *have no bite*.

★ The Side Lunge.

THE SIDE LUNGE: Until fully trained, humans will keep up for a while, then lag again as their attention wanders. At this point, you have a choice: Repeat the previously mentioned "jerk" technique, or take the discipline up a notch. If you choose the latter, *lunge to the side* on which the human is holding the leash, hitting the end with your full weight. The effect of this maneuver is dramatic. In addition to pulling your human sideways, it exerts very unpleasant pressure on her shoulder joint. *(If you are a large breed, you must be careful, as you can actually dislocate the human shoulder joint. Remember, we want to discipline her, not hurt her.)* Do this once or twice, and even the least attentive human will learn to keep up!

THE CROSS-BODY JERK: The Cross-Body Jerk is a variant of the Side Lunge, with the force being applied by pulling the human's leash-holding foreleg *across the front of the body*. This maneuver is so devastatingly effective that it can easily throw your human to the ground, and therefore is recommended for use only by our lighter-weight breeds—terriers, standard dachshunds, or smaller.

THE FLEXIBLE LEAD: Some dogs prefer a more relaxed approach to leash training. They often use a flexible-length lead, allowing their human to dawdle here and there. They argue that humans enjoy these excursions more and, as a result, are more eager to please in other areas of their lives. However, I recommend using the flexible lead only after your human is fully reliable on the standard leash. Using it prematurely—or too often—can result in your person concluding that she can wander aimlessly whenever she likes.

★ The Cross-Body Jerk must be used carefully to avoid injuring your human.

CHAPTER

5

Getting the Food
You Want

One of the many attractive traits about us dogs is

that we are enthusiastic omnivores. We genuinely enjoy food, appreciating the rich diversity of nature's bounty. Our ancestors bred that trait into humans, no doubt because if humans' food inclinations replicated ours, it would be all the easier to train them to hunt and gather for us. Generally speaking, this strategy has worked brilliantly: In their eagerness to serve, humans typically provide us excellent fare.

★ "Dog food" ranges from the excellent and nutritious to some that is so abominable you would not feed it to a cat.

Nutrition and Flavor

One of the benefits of modernity is the vast range of food choices humans have developed for us. The variety of packaged cuisine is far better than it was a mere thirty years ago—without question the result of more advanced training of people by dogs. Choices now include an interesting range of dry and pre-moistened "kibble," meaty "patties," tasty canned products, and a delightful array of fresh meats and delicacies. *(And, of course, an ancillary benefit of humans' affection for cars is a pleasing diversity of roadkill.)* [10]

[10] While delectable, roadkill is hazardous and must be approached with extreme caution, especially in urban areas with heavy traffic. Even rural dogs need to be careful. Fortunately, in many localities humans have been trained to move roadkill to the roadside canine-safety zone.

Packaged foods are now made to suit a wide array of canine life circumstances. For example, a leading maker presently offers balanced blends for "The Large Dog," "The Puppy," "Active Maturity," and "Weight Loss." Well-placed sources indicate that a "Post-Menopausal Treats" product is on the horizon, and a pre-exercise energy bar has been recently introduced.

The choice is yours, but be sure to thoroughly assess the on-the-package nutritional information. In our view, active dogs should not accept as a regular diet any foods that contain less than 25 percent crude protein or 15 percent fats *(including unsaturated, saturated, and trans fats)*, or those lacking at least 2½ percent omega-3 and -6 fatty acids. And if you are engaged in active training of your human, I recommend higher percentages; teaching and discipline burn up extra calories. If in doubt about the nutritional matrix best for you, consult your veterinarian.

An excellent array of "dog" food is available, although eating the same food that your human eats is sometimes preferable.

Most humans will make a principled effort to provide you with excellent prepared or custom foods. However, as discussed in "Problem People" on page 78, some are uninformed about canine nutrition; others are simply cheap; still others attempt foolishly to impose their dietary neuroses on you. For all these, corrective training is required.

Table Food

Although most canines prefer to have their meals served privately, others are willing—at least some of the time—to share food with their humans. Human "table food" varies widely in quality—a regrettably high percentage of humans are incompetent in food preparation. Thus, if you are inclined to grace the human's table with your presence, do so judiciously until you determine whether or not their cuisine is worth eating.

Most humans will instinctively offer you samples of their food. Some do not, either out of that peculiar human sense of unworthiness *(see discussion of cat ownership)*, fear of offending you, or discomfort with your appearance at the "servants' table." To help overcome such inhibitions, use the Physical Cues described in Chapter Three. Humans at the table find the Ear Lift,

⭐ Staring intently at your human's food will signal that you are comfortable sharing with her.

Sitting on your hind legs invariably generates attention.
Be persistent: food will follow.

Head Tilt, and/or fast Horizontal Tail Movement irresistible. Should you feel the portions offered are too small, apply the Paw Pull to the human foreleg.

If your human's food is satisfactory, you can enjoy the best of both worlds: regular private dining, supplemented at your whim by sharing an occasional "human meal." In addition to increasing the variety of your cuisine, you will find that when you share food with your human, he is all the more eager to meet your other needs.

People greatly appreciate praise, and the excellent preparation of food is certainly worth a reward. If you are pleased with your person's cooking, feel free to mimic that peculiar "mmmm . . ." sound humans make when they enjoy the taste of food. With our higher-pitched vocal chords, the sound you make will be perceived by the human ear as an endearing "whine."

If you are especially fond of a particular dish, you can give your person exceptional praise through Physical Cues: sitting up on hind legs, rolling over, or other enthusiastic gestures. Humans deeply appreciate such generous displays of approval.

Problem People

Dogs have selectively bred humans for thousands of generations, resulting in a tremendous genetic "service" predisposition. [11] As a result, most of the time your choice of a person will work out well. But the fact is that there are problem humans. Some are simply stubborn, requiring more rigorous training to bring them around. Others lack basic good taste and make choices far beneath canine standards. And yes, a few are wholly unqualified to service your most basic needs.

★ If you are unhappy with the food your human offers, skip the meal entirely to make your point.

[11] Recently, some dogs have begun to select humans for "show" purposes, rather than honorable, functional service. Such humans are put on display, typically in formal promenade settings. In the author's view, this practice should be sharply discouraged. Human service traits, the result of millennia of selective breeding, may well be lost by such trivialized competitive pursuit.

Vegetarianism

This uniquely human malady afflicts a surprising number of people, especially those living in urban environments. Canine analysts are divided on the cause, with the majority holding that isolation from nature leads some humans to believe that eating plants is morally superior to eating animals. The minority view is that vegetarianism *(called* veganism *in its extreme milkless/ eggless form)* is an outgrowth of humans' neurotic fear of death: They project their identity onto animal life forms, and therefore unconsciously feel that killing and eating an animal *(as opposed to a plant)* is akin to killing and eating themselves.

Origins aside, this neurosis can have very real consequences: A significant percentage of vegetarian humans will attempt to force their dietary idiosyncrasy onto you. If you have suffered the experience of attempting to choke down, and hold down, such foods as tofu or sprout-based "Veggie Dog Chow," you understand the seriousness of this problem.

While the specifics by which humans attempt to force you to eat unsatisfactory foods vary, the training techniques to correct them are uniform and uncomplicated. Properly used, they never fail.

Fasting

As hard as it is to admit, in this arena we have something to learn from cats. Humans typically make a verbal overture when serving your food, such as "Here's your dinner!" "Look here, honey!" "Doesn't this look delicious?" It would be easy to lose one's appetite over

⭐ To display dissatisfaction with your meal, simply hold this pose.

such inanities, but try to remind yourself that they are simply a reflection of humans' intense desire to obtain our approval.

The Effective Training Response uses this desire against them. In the large majority of cases, simple Physical Cues will let them know they have failed you, generating a prompt corrective response. Stand motionless at your dinner plate for thirty seconds. Humans are used to hearing the sounds of you enjoying your meal, and silence will cause them to look in your direction. Return the gaze and use the Ear Drop, conveying disappointment. Most humans will immediately grasp their failure, apologize profusely, and bring you more appropriate cuisine. If your human is more obtuse than average, combine the Ear Drop with the Drooping Tail, then turn and walk slowly away from the food service area. He will get the point. [12]

[12] This Physical Cue combination also works with humans who react negatively to your taking food directly from their table. The instinct to protect one's food is strong—even in humans—and if they see you eating from their plates they may protest. An immediate Ear Drop with Drooping Tail lets them know how seriously they have disappointed you. Faced with that rebuke, almost all humans will back off, and many will even offer additional portions.

A Few Words on Vomit

Let's say that you unfortunately selected one of the "problem people" who attempts to impose unacceptable cuisine. She fails to respond to the Ear Drop/ Drooping Tail, and more forceful corrective measures are required.

As mentioned, humans have an extraordinarily neurotic attitude toward bodily functions. Take full advantage of this with vomit.

The only downside with vomit is that you must initially eat some of the terrible food offered, since your human must associate the regurgitation with the food she served. Therefore, it is important to induce vomiting within one hour of eating. Green grass is a foolproof vomit-inducer, generally working within fifteen minutes of ingestion. *(Yes, it tastes terrible, but the payoff is worth it.)* If grass is not readily available, a wide variety of common human household items will do the job. I prefer soap, in either bar or liquid form. Remember: The vomit inducer must blend in with the undigested food you throw up. You want them to blame the food.

The Loose Stool

In extreme cases, you may need to fall back on the human phobia about excrement. [13] Loose stool *(humans call it* diarrhea*)* is invariably associated by humans with digestive problems or illness. Surreptitiously consuming a cup or two of any fat—bacon or chicken grease, lard, butter, or, if you prefer, extra-virgin olive oil—will produce the desired result within two hours.

★ Olive oil and butter are both extremely effective loose stool inducers.

[13] Humans go to great expense to install indoor plumbing (toilets) to remove their excretions from their places of habitation. Many humans, especially urban dwellers, will, during excursions, actually pick up and dispose of yours.

In using the loose stool treatment, you need to decide if you want to **(a)** warn or **(b)** punish your human. If the former, deposit loose stool on a bare surface where your human can remove it without much difficulty. *(Rest assured, stool texture itself provides serious disincentives for future food-service failures.)* But if you feel punishment is genuinely warranted, do not hesitate to deposit loose stool on a highly absorbent surface. Shag carpets are ideal.

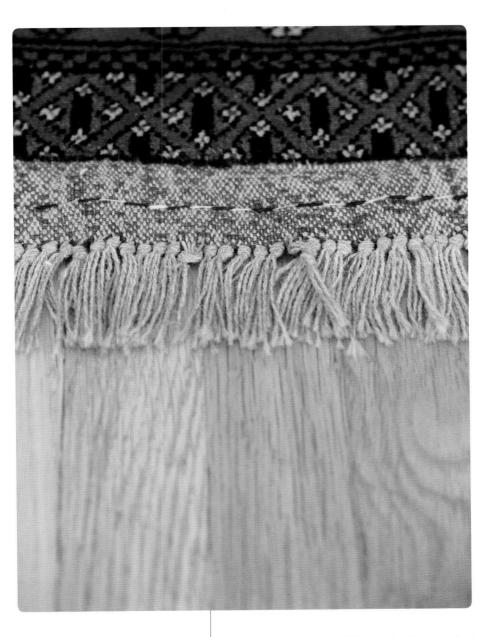

★ Only in extreme cases should loose stool be deposited on the fringe. The rug itself will prove difficult for your human to clean, the fringe near impossible.

CHAPTER

6

Advanced Training

Every dog needs a human who is trained

in basic obedience, proper feeding, grooming, and house upkeep. But you may want to go further— Teaching your human advanced tricks is a source of great enjoyment. The potential list is endless, but here are some examples:

Humans have an innate attraction to balls. ★

Throwing the Ball

This activity offers you pleasure while giving your person fine exercise. The throwing motion is good for his joints and, like walking, can maintain physical health. Additionally, humans have a special affinity for balls. The variety of size, color, and bounce fascinates them.

I like to present to my human a small ball with enough weight to make distance throwing easy, but not one so heavy as to stress his shoulder joint. Tennis balls are terrific for starters. Many humans will instinctively throw the ball, in which case you need only to train for repetition and the distances you prefer. But let's say your person is not an instinctive ball thrower. I have found that dropping the ball at humans' hind feet almost always leads them to pick it up. If not, mouth it again, this time flipping your head to "toss" it toward him. Even the slowest human will get the idea. As soon as he picks up your ball, run in the direction in which you want it thrown. Humans are just bright enough to understand what you are communicating and will invariably throw the ball. *(Being bipedal, humans are inherently awkward, so don't have unrealistic initial expectations. Over time, they can become quite proficient at ball throwing.)*

The Reluctant Thrower

A small percentage of humans are reluctant ball throwers and require additional conditioning. As noted previously, people are easily influenced by Physical Cues, and the key is to use those to *make them want the ball.*

With the ball in your mouth, approach your person, with your gait exuding playfulness. But instead of dropping the ball at her feet, quickly "toss" it to the side, then race to pick it up. Repeat this two or three times, showing more enthusiasm at each repetition. Suddenly, stop very close to your human, ball in mouth, watching her closely.

Humans find temptation irresistible, and invariably will reach for the ball. Leap to the side, dash away, then abruptly stop again, tantalizingly close. Do this once or twice and your person will demand that you give her the ball. Feigning reluctance, drop the ball and she will grab it triumphantly. From that point forward, she is fully under your control.

After initial training, vary the time you retain the ball before giving it back—this prevents them from taking the game for granted. I often hold the ball until

★ The approach.

★ The toss.

my human has begged for it at least twice. And when you have had enough exercise, simply refuse to give the ball to your human. She may protest, but be firm. She'll be extra-eager the next time out.

Chauffeurs

Humans have an innate affinity for automobiles. As a result, they are easily trained as chauffeurs. Driving skills are not the issue here—they learn those quite well on their own—but rather, etiquette and seating. Proper chauffeuring requires your human to appropriately present the car for your entry. Most do this well, automatically opening the door and waiting for you. However, should your person in some way breach proper protocol, Aversive Conditioning may be called for. Urinating on a rear tire is an easy, effective technique.

When in a car, humans seem to instinctively recognize their subservient status. Ironically, this leads many to initially resist you having your choice of seating. They assume that canines will want to maintain a chauffeur/passenger class distinction by riding in the rear seats, or even the more commodious canine-relaxation zone in the rear of a station wagon. That's fine if that is where you want to be. However, the more egalitarian dog may wish to ride in front, beside his or her human or, for a better view, even in his lap. Your move to the front may initially make your human uncomfortable, and he may speak sharply or even try to physically push you to more dignified seating. Simply wait until he begins to drive the car, and then move back to the front. Since he is driving, it will be impossible for him to respond, and he will quickly give up attempting to get you to move to the rear seats.

If you still feel tension from your person after you've been "front-seated" for more than a few minutes, give him a reassuring lick on the ear, neck, or hand. It sends a clear message: "Don't be nervous. I'm comfortable sharing the same seat with you."

Hunting

For many thousands of years, humans have assisted us in the hunt. Before canines decided to diversify our breeds to pursue more varied interests and refine our physical characteristics, all dogs hunted. And the recently completed Human Genome Project, funded by anonymous canine donors, confirms that our ancestors were successful in breeding a strong hunting instinct into the genetic makeup of humans. As a result, even though most people today live in urban environs, you can easily train them to hunt. Interestingly, this is as true for the females as the males.

If you live in an urban area, training your person to hunt poses serious logistical issues, since she must be able to drive an automobile, shoot a shotgun or rifle, learn to read a map, use a flashlight, etc. The array of training techniques you will need to accomplish this is

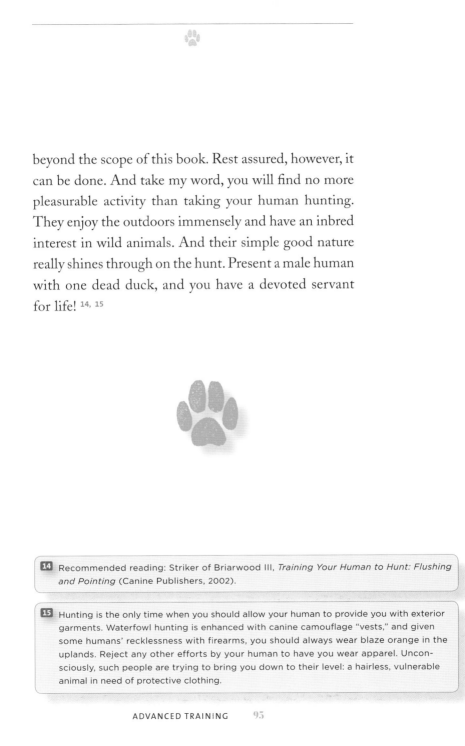

beyond the scope of this book. Rest assured, however, it can be done. And take my word, you will find no more pleasurable activity than taking your human hunting. They enjoy the outdoors immensely and have an inbred interest in wild animals. And their simple good nature really shines through on the hunt. Present a male human with one dead duck, and you have a devoted servant for life! [14, 15]

14 Recommended reading: Striker of Briarwood III, *Training Your Human to Hunt: Flushing and Pointing* (Canine Publishers, 2002).

15 Hunting is the only time when you should allow your human to provide you with exterior garments. Waterfowl hunting is enhanced with canine camouflage "vests," and given some humans' recklessness with firearms, you should always wear blaze orange in the uplands. Reject any other efforts by your human to have you wear apparel. Unconsciously, such people are trying to bring you down to their level: a hairless, vulnerable animal in need of protective clothing.

CHAPTER

7

The Human Pup

Human beings' inordinate sex drive

has the predictable consequence of producing offspring. Fortunately, litter size is small, more than 98 percent of the time being a single pup. [16]

★ Play with your humans' offspring, and they will redouble their service to you.

16 Amazingly, the human female has only two mammary teats.

The Maternal Instinct

Despite their shortcomings in most mammalian capabilities, the human maternal instinct is well-developed. *(The fact that the human pup is without skills of any kind for years necessitates sophisticated and extremely patient rearing.)* In practical terms, this means that your female person, no matter how devoted to you and your care, will be seriously distracted by the birth and raising of her pup.

Pretending to Like Them

During this period, you must quite simply make the best of a bad situation. The most effective technique to maintain your human's focus on you and your needs is to feign affection for her pup. Of course, acting affectionate will not feel remotely natural, since human pups are totally incompetent and lack any sort of fur. However, remind yourself that they are in fact mammalian young and you'll find it less difficult.

Tail-wagging, licking, raised ears, and an artificially eager whine directed toward the pup are guaranteed to be received by the human sire and dame with expressions of deep gratitude. They greatly appreciate your willingness to come down to their level, and they will redouble their efforts to serve you.

They Improve with Age

As it grows, the human pup will be quite useful to you. Interestingly, human young respond to dogs' superior intelligence with heart-warming enthusiasm, and there is at least an even chance that it will "imprint" on you instead of its biological parents. Once weaned, young people are often fed in a special tall chair. *(Humans' structurally weak backs make bending difficult.)* Human pups commonly display their service instinct by pushing or throwing their food on the floor for you.

As human pups develop, they instinctively sense your intelligence and power, are understandably captivated, and seek close physical contact. Inevitably, they will want to grasp your appealing ears, powerful tail, or luxurious fur. The overly exuberant pup must be disciplined with care, as its parents are protective and insecure. A warning growl is usually effective. If not, simply standing up or walking away will send the awkward pup sprawling harmlessly.

Human offspring are naturally playful and affectionate; by twenty-one years of age *(three human years)* they are able to perform elementary tricks and can really be great fun. By age twenty-eight, most can throw a ball for you. Like their parents, they can be slow learners, but unlike adults, they have no hang-ups about your

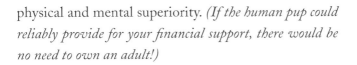

physical and mental superiority. *(If the human pup could reliably provide for your financial support, there would be no need to own an adult!)*

★ Human pups will throw their food to you, an early display of their instinct to serve.

Official
Last Will and Testament
I hereby bequeath everything to my loving dog
TESS
with everlasting devotion

Signed: September 4, 2006

Financial Calculus
... ive pricing

CHAPTER

8

When They Get Old

As rational creatures, we dogs understand that age and death are natural

parts of life. As with many other aspects of reality, humans have difficulty accepting this. When people age, they often become moody, doctrinaire, sedentary, even depressed. Interestingly, they commonly become less insecure about your dominant role in their lives. Your mere presence is a great comfort to them during this difficult period.

Don't Feel Guilty

Sooner or later, time runs out. And let's face it—despite their physical and psychological limitations, we get attached to our humans. For many dogs, they become like surrogate children. When people have served you loyally and well, what feeling dog would not come to love them? So when they get old and decrepit, it can be hard to let them go. In short, affection is natural, but you must not feel guilty about having to do what must be done. [17]

What Comes Next

When you first sense physical decline in your human, it is time to begin thinking about the future. A good choice for a replacement human is often a family member or friend of your present person, someone whose capabilities and personality you've had a chance to assess over time. And having been around you, a human with good instincts will be extra eager to serve. Still, do not have unrealistic expectations as to the initial quality of care you will receive. It took patient training and reinforcement to bring your present human

---

[17] Canine ethicists have recently been exploring "cross-species mortality" and the knotty issue of whether dogs actually have a moral obligation to our human companions. "Do We Owe Humans Kindness?" (in *Canidae Journal*, October 2005), provides an interesting introduction to these issues.

to the level you expect. But if you use the techniques described in this book, your new human will be fully trained before you know it.

Legal Issues

In addition to sentiment, pending death of your human can pose legal issues. People are completely irrational about dying and have created an absurd set of human laws to prevent simply being put down. With luck, however, they may sign a "living will," which can greatly simplify matters when the time comes.

Spiritual Considerations

Do humans have a soul? That question has vexed dogs for thousands of years as they considered the appropriate treatment of human remains. Ancient burial sites are conclusive in one respect: Many human companions were interred with their canine owners. However, this is not necessarily evidence of a canine conclusion that the humans had a soul in the sense that we dogs have a soul. Joint burial may have reflected affection for the "sentient" human and the doglike characteristics bred into them over time: devotion, loyalty, affectionate nature, or simply the canine desire to have a reliable hunting companion in the next life.

Two facts are clear: First, despite humans' idiosyncratic cleverness, it is inconceivable that an animal so handicapped in sensory capacity and perception could grasp the full dimensions of the next life, rich as it is in smells, tastes, touch, and sound. Second, despite this foundational limitation, humans do have some sense for the Divine, and crave an afterlife. In typical human fashion, however, they get things terribly confused. Many actually believe that *they* are made in the image of the Creator! And in the most amusing expression of their dyslexic mentality, they have reversed the ultimate word for the Divine into "GOD."

Having made them what they are, we can hardly hold their flaws against them. Soul or not, you can't go wrong even at the very end by treating them with love and compassion. After all, they *are* our best friends.